—REGULATIONS—
FINES ARE CHARGED FOR OVERDUE AND/OR
LOST LIBRARY MATERIALS; AND, IN ACCOR-
DANCE WITH BOARD POLICY 8741, "GRADES
TRANSCRIPTS, DEGREES, AND REGISTRATION
PRIVILEGES SHALL BE WITHHELD UNTIL ALL
LIBRARY BOOKS OR OTHER LIBRARY MATERIALS
ARE RETURNED (TO THE LIBRARY CIRCULATION
DESK)."

Contra Costa College Library
2600 Mission Bell Drive
San Pablo, California 94806

Field Marshal Erwin Rommel was in every sense a "fighting general." Always to the forefront with his leading troops, he possessed all the qualities essential in a military leader – courage, drive, imagination and determination. In the fast-moving desert war, Rommel's ability to get the best out of his men led the Africa Corps from strength to strength. Whenever the enemy was unprepared, Rommel did not theorize, he struck – in Cyrenaica, at Gazala, at Tobruk.

Greatly respected by his own men, Hitler's "Desert Fox" was also regarded with something like affection by his enemies. In this new *History Makers* title, F. H. Gregory shows how this stern, rather old fashioned patriot lived almost entirely for soldiering, caring nothing for luxuries and happy in the most frugal conditions. True to a soldier's code of honour, he cared little for politics and was never a member of the Nazi Party. Indeed, Rommel had nothing but contempt for the sinister trappings of the Third Reich – the brownshirts, the S.S., the Gestapo.

It was this sense of honour, his great love for Germany and concern for the fate of the German people, that led Rommel into conflict with Hitler, and to the final tragedy of his enforced suicide.

WAYLAND HISTORY MAKERS

Rommel

F. H. Gregory

WAYLAND PUBLISHERS

More Wayland History Makers

frontispiece: Field Marshal Erwin
Rommel.

SBN 85340 394 5
Copyright © 1974 by Wayland Publishers Limited
49 Lansdowne Place, Hove, East Sussex BN3 1HF
First published in 1974 by Wayland Publishers Limited
Second impression 1978
Filmset in 'Monophoto' Baskerville and printed offset litho by
Page Bros (Norwich) Ltd, Norwich, England

Contents

List of Illustrations

1. The Final Choice

On 13th October, 1944, at noon, two German generals, Burgdorf and Maisel, arrived at the home of Field Marshal Erwin Rommel and asked to speak to him in private. The interview lasted nearly an hour, after which Rommel went upstairs to speak to his wife.

"As he entered the room," she explained later, "there was so strange and terrible an expression on his face that I exclaimed at once, 'What is the matter with you? What has happened? Are you ill?' He looked at me and replied: 'I have come to say goodbye. In a quarter of an hour I shall be dead . . . They suspect me of having taken part in the attempt to kill Hitler. It seems my name was on [the conspirators'] list to be President of the Reich . . . The Fuehrer has given me the choice of taking poison or being dragged before the People's Court. They have brought the poison. They say it will take only three seconds to act.'" Frau Rommel pleaded with her husband to go before the Court, but he would have none of it: "I would not be afraid to be tried in public, for I can defend everything I have done. But I know I should never reach Berlin alive."

After saying his farewells to his wife and his son, Manfred, Rommel explained the situation to Captain Aldinger, his personal aide and long-standing friend. Aldinger suggested one last desperate move: "I told him that he must at least make an attempt to escape.

Opposite **Field Marshal Erwin Rommel with his wife and son.**

Why could we not try to shoot our way out together? We had been in as bad places before and got away. 'It's no good, my friend,' he said, 'this is it. All the streets are blocked with S.S. cars and the Gestapo are all around the house' . . . I said we could at least shoot Burgdorf and Maisel. 'No,' said Rommel, 'they have their orders. Besides, I have my wife and Manfred to think of.' Then he told me that he had been promised that no harm should come to them if he took the first choice . . . 'I have spoken to my wife and made up my mind,' he said. 'I will never allow myself to be hanged by that man Hitler. I planned no murder. I only tried to serve my country, as I have done all my life, but now this is what I must do.' "

And so the Desert Fox drove off to his death with Hitler's emissaries. Twenty-five minutes later the telephone rang. Aldinger answered. Rommel was dead, he was told, he had had a haemorrhage, a brain storm in the car.

This marked the beginning of one of history's most elaborate charades. Few people were to know what really happened to the Field Marshal until after the war. When Rommel's death was announced the public were made to believe he had died of war wounds. Hitler even had the effrontery to send a message of condolence to Rommel's widow. Then came the state funeral with all its pomp and circumstance. Field Marshal von Rundstedt gave the funeral ovation. It ended with the words, "His heart belonged to the Fuehrer." A bitter irony.

Above **Rommel's flag-draped coffin being carried from the Town Hall of Ulm to be placed onto the gun carriage.**

2. The Son of a Schoolmaster

It would have seemed most unlikely to anyone who knew Rommel as a boy that he would ever become a soldier. His sister described him as "a very gentle and docile child." He was small for his age and showed no interest in games. Nor did he show any signs of mental ability – he was uninterested in books and inattentive and lazy at school.

Erwin Johannes Eugen Rommel was born on 15th November, 1891, in Heidenheim. This town is situated in what is now the southern part of West Germany and was then the German Kingdom of Württemburg. Erwin's mother, Helena, was the daughter of Karl von Luz, the President of the Government of Württemburg. His father was also called Erwin Rommel, a schoolmaster particularly distinguished in mathematics. An ability in mathematics was something young Rommel also showed, but not until he reached adolescence, at which time he became more energetic and developed a practical character very different from the lethargic schoolboy of earlier years. He began to enjoy physical as well as mental activities – he not only passed his exams but also spent many hours bicycling and skiing in his spare time.

Although he now had a temperament suitable for soldiering his choice of a career in the Army was not an obvious one. The Rommels were respectable middle

> " 'Tough' is the adjective most obviously appropriate to Rommel of the Afrika Korps, but as a small boy Erwin Rommel was the reverse of tough. 'Small for his age, '[said his sister]' he had a white skin and hair so pale that we called him the white bear.' " *Desmond Young. Rommel.*

Opposite **Danzig, where Rommel attended the War Academy.**

13

class people but, being middle class, they had no connections in the Army. At that time most German officers came from landowning families and particularly from the Prussian aristocracy. Officers of noble birth or with good family connections were favoured for promotion; Rommel was at a great disadvantage.

His military career began in July, 1910, when he joined the 124th Infantry Regiment. As an officer cadet he had to serve in the ranks before being given a command. After eight months in the ranks he was sent to the War Academy at Danzig. During his time in Danzig he met his future wife, Lucie Maria Mollin.

At the War Academy Rommel was faced with examinations which he did not find easy – he passed them only by working hard. Finally in January, 1912, he received his commission as an officer, and returned to his regiment with a rank of 2nd Lieutenant.

During the following two years Rommel did not distinguish himself in any way. He was the serious type, he did not smoke or drink and was rather strict with his subordinates. Although he was quite strong, he was still rather short. There was nothing to suggest that he would become one of the world's most famous generals.

Eventually, however, he was given the chance to show what he was worth. By August, 1914, the 124th Infantry Regiment had donned its battle dress and was on the march. The First World War had begun.

"Then, when he was in his 'teens, he suddenly woke up . . . He lost his dreamy abstracted air and reverted to the type of Württemberg, 'the home of common sense in Germany.' He became hard-headed and practical – and very careful of his money, another Württemberger characteristic."
Desmond Young. Rommel.

Above **Some aristocratic members of the Prussian Army.**

3. Rommel goes to War

The period covering the First World War is remembered as the era of trench warfare, but this type of war was not expected by the military leaders of the time. They thought the next war would be a war of mobility which would only last a few months. And indeed the war *was* mobile – at first. The German Army literally swept through Belgium and northern France pushing back the French forces. However, their master plan failed and they were checked before they could reach Paris. Both armies then became entrenched and remained more or less static for the next three years.

It was during this first period of mobile warfare that Rommel saw his first action. In mid August, 1914, his regiment began an attack on French positions. At five o'clock one morning the Germans advanced across the fields. A thick fog lay on the ground. Soon Rommel's platoon came under French fire. Rommel and his men charged towards the enemy but the French escaped before they could reach them. Having lost sight of the rest of his regiment in the fog, but seeing the footprints of the retreating French in the soil, he led his men in pursuit. They came to a group of farm buildings on the outskirts of the town of Bleid. Rommel left his platoon to take cover behind a hedge and went ahead with three men to reconnoitre.

They proceeded cautiously. Looking round the corner

Opposite **German troops in a trench, France, 1916.**

17

of a building, Rommel saw between fifteen and twenty French soldiers standing in the road – they were chatting idly and drinking coffee. Rommel did not doubt that he should attack, but should he bring up the rest of the platoon? He did not hesitate, in a moment the four of them had jumped out from behind the building and opened fire. They stood only twenty yards from their enemy, a very short range for their deadly rifle fire. Some of the enemy soldiers fell to the ground dead or wounded, but most of them quickly took cover and returned fire. The exchange of fire continued until the enemy was reduced to about ten in number. Then Rommel signalled his men to rush and with a yell the four Germans dashed forward. But suddenly more French soldiers started firing from the windows of nearby houses. Rommel and his men were forced to beat a hasty retreat – a successful one, too, as they all returned safely to their platoon.

Again Rommel was faced with a decision – should he wait for the rest of the regiment or continue the attack with his platoon? He decided on the latter. They burnt down a farmhouse and captured those French

Right German troops in a French village, August, 1918.

18

soldiers who were taking cover in it. This Rommel did at the cost of only a few men slightly wounded.

Rommel's first engagement with the enemy is well worth thinking about. If he had bought up the whole platoon instead of attacking the unwary French soldiers with only three men he *might* have killed even more of the enemy. But is this likely? The Frenchmen might equally well have heard the platoon approaching and been alerted, or they might simply have finished their coffee and moved off before the German platoon arrived. Undoubtedly, Rommel's decision was the right one, it was also typical of the decisions he would make commanding much larger forces in the years to come. Whenever the enemy was unprepared and vulnerable he struck at them, he never lost the opportunity by waiting for his own reinforcements.

There followed numerous other battles in which Rommel showed his tactical skill and his powers of physical endurance. He also had tremendous courage, which he displayed quite alarmingly towards the end of September, 1914. His company was attacking the French in a wood when they came under heavy fire. As the casualties mounted Rommel found it increasingly difficult to urge his men forward. Having spotted five French soldiers he advanced toward them. After shooting two of the enemy he found that his rifle was empty. His own men were far behind him and could be of no help – so he charged the remaining Frenchmen with his bayonet. "As I rushed forwards," he later wrote, "the enemy fired. Struck, I went head over heels and wound up a few paces in front of the enemy. A bullet entering sideways had shattered my upper left leg, and blood spurted from a wound as large as my fist."

Soon he was on his way to a field hospital. A few days later he was decorated with the Iron Cross, Second Class.

"Finally, scarcely twenty paces ahead I saw five Frenchmen firing from the standing position. Instantly my gun was at my shoulder. Two Frenchmen standing one behind the other dropped to the ground as my rifle cracked. I was still faced by three of them. Apparently my men sought shelter behind me and couldn't help me. I fired again. The rifle missed fire. I quickly opened the magazine and found it empty. The nearness of the enemy left no time for reloading, nor was any shelter close at hand . . . The bayonet was my only hope."
Erwin Rommel. Infantry Attacks.

4. Pour le Mérite

Rommel returned to the front after his discharge from hospital in January, 1915. By that time both sides had constructed a complex of trenches which stretched from the English Channel to the Swiss border. The trenches were strong defensive positions. Barbed wire entanglements in front protected the defenders from infantry attacks while dug-outs offered protection from shell fire. Offensive actions, whether on a small or a large scale, were usually costly failures. But Rommel showed himself capable of making a successful attack with few losses among the small groups of men under his command.

In 1917, after being promoted to 1st Lieutenant and transferred to the Württemburg Mountain Battalion, he was sent to the Eastern front. Here, fighting against the Rumanians in the Carpathian mountains, Rommel once again showed his skill – despite much hard fighting his attacks were successful.

But it was on the Italian front that Rommel would excel himself as a commander. The Italians, allied to the French and British, were engaged in an offensive action against the Austrians (Germany's allies). After eleven battles in the Isonzo Valley the Italians had made little progress. But the Austrians feared a serious defeat in the next battle and asked for German support. The German High Command sent troops, including the Württemburg Mountain Battalion, and planned the

Opposite **Austrian soldiers tracking down Italians in the mountains.**

counter attack that would drive the Italians back to where they had started.

The German attack took place near Tolmein. The main Italian defences in this area consisted of trenches along a number of mountain peaks. From these trenches the Italians looked down upon the valley and the river Isonzo. After overcoming the defences across the valley the main German forces began an assault up the slopes. This frontal attack on the Italian positions involved a great deal of hard fighting even for the Germans. The Italians had dug trench after trench along the mountainside, each one fortified with thick barbed wire entanglements. When the Germans forced their way across one trench the Italians abandoned it and fell back on the trench immediately behind.

While his fellow officers were attacking in the normal way Rommel was using unconventional tactics. When he had forced his way across a fortified trench he quickly pushed his detachment forward rather than waiting to consolidate his gain. This way he often reached the reserve trenches before the enemy could fall back to them. He also took every opportunity to surprise the enemy by attacking in unexpected places – as a result his men often got through the wire before the Italians realized what was happening! In this way Rommel's detachment managed to penetrate a number of lines at the cost of only a few casualties. The Italians brought up reinforcements, but instead of counter attacking Rommel's detachment they merely dug themselves more trenches and prepared to block his further advance. Rommel, true to form, found a way round these trenches and led his mountain troops into the Italian rear.

Two miles behind the enemy lines Rommel's detachment took up position on one of the supply routes. He later described what happened to the

"In the battles from October 24th to 26th, 1917, various Italian regiments regarded their situation as hopeless and gave up the fight prematurely when they saw themselves attacked on the flank or rear. The Italian commanders lacked resolution. They were not accustomed to our supple offensive tactics, and besides, they did not have their men well enough in hand."
Erwin Rommel. Infantry Attacks.

23

surprised Italians using the road: "From north and south single soldiers and vehicles came unsuspectingly towards us. They were politely received at the sharp curves of the road by a few mountain soldiers and taken prisoner. Everyone was having fun and there was no shooting . . . soon we had more than a hundred prisoners and fifty vehicles. Business was booming." Better was to follow; a column of enemy infantry came down the road and after ten minutes of fighting with the 150 men of Rommel's detachment they surrendered. This added fifty Italian officers and two thousand Italian soldiers to Rommel's bag of prisoners.

The next day Rommel began to attack on the Italian defensive line along the mountain peaks. The Italians, being fully occupied by the main German attack up the slopes of the valley, were unpleasantly surprised by Rommel's detachment coming at them from the rear. Rommel went from peak to peak along the Italian line, and each of these strong points collapsed without much resistance. The key to the Italian position was Mount Matajur. By the time Rommel reached it his detachment had become spread out. Few of his troops, burdened with heavy packs, could keep up with their leader over this difficult mountain terrain. Thus Rommel had only a handful of men with him when he saw a vast mass of Italians ahead – 1,500 of them. Rommel's small and exhausted force could easily have been overwhelmed if the Italians had attacked. But they did not – they just stood there horrified, watching the Germans advancing from their rear. Rommel was determined to take decisive action before the Italians did. He walked towards them shouting and waving his handkerchief as a signal to them to surrender. The fully armed Italians remained immobile. Rommel continued walking towards them; if they had opened fire he could not have escaped, if he had stopped they might have realized how weak the German forces were. "I came to within 150 yards of the enemy," Rommel later recalled; "Suddenly the mass began to move and in the ensuing panic, swept its resisting officers along downhill. Most of the soldiers threw their weapons away and hundreds hurried to me. In an instant I was surrounded and hoisted on Italian shoulders. 'Evviva Germania!' sounded from a thousand throats. An Italian officer who hesitated to surrender was shot down by his own troops."

Further up Mount Matajur the Rommel detachment encountered the soldiers of a crack Italian regiment, the second regiment of the Salerno Brigade, but after a brief fight they also surrendered. Rommel reached the summit of Mount Matajur shortly afterwards, and with this the Italian defensive position was shattered. The Italian Army now began to retreat in earnest. The nine thousand Italian soldiers whom Rommel had captured were marched off to prison camps. This tremendous success had cost the Rommel detachment only six men dead and thirty wounded. For this great achievement Rommel was awarded the Pour le Mérite, Germany's highest military decoration.

Not long afterwards, and much to his regret, Rommel was recalled from front line service and given an administrative position until the end of the war.

"Before us – scarcely three hundred yards away – stood the 2nd regiment of the Salerno Brigade. It was assembling and laying down its arms. Deeply moved, the regimental commander sat at the roadside surrounded by his officers and wept with rage and shame at the insubordination of the soldiers of his once-proud regiment. Quickly, before the Italians saw my small numbers, I separated the 35 officers from the 1,200 men so far assembled, and I sent the latter down the Matajur road at the double . . . The captured colonel fumed with rage when he saw that we were only a handful of German soldiers."
Erwin Rommel. Infantry Attacks.

5. From 1918 to 1939

After Germany had been defeated in 1918 Rommel chose to stay in the Army. Under the Allied peace terms the size of the German Army was limited to 100,000 men – a fraction of its former size. Its officers were a small group of highly competent military commanders among whom Rommel could easily find a place.

In 1918, Rommel was twenty-seven years old. He had established himself as an exceptional soldier. Not only had he proved his ability to lead men in daring and imaginative thrusts into enemy territory, he was also skilled in defence, being able to make his men keep their positions under heavy attack. In the Rumanian campaign he had at times large numbers of soldiers under his command and had shown himself more than equal to the task of handling them. He was also capable of remarkable physical endurance – he could go for days without sleeping or eating, he could out-match his men and could fight on even when sick or wounded.

Rommel's activities during the period between the wars are of little interest. As he grew older he acquired higher rank, and he seems to have enjoyed the peace-time Army life. In 1916 he had married Lucie Maria Mollin. He and his wife now lived comparatively uneventful lives. In 1928 their first and only son was born.

Opposite **Hitler reviewing his troops in Warsaw after the surrender of the city, 1939.**

It was during these years that Rommel wrote his book, *Infantry Attacks*. The Nazi Party was in power when the book was published in 1937. Their leader, and now the leader of the German people, was Adolf Hitler. He read Rommel's book and liked it. As a result he had Rommel appointed commander of his personal escort battalion. When, in 1939, the Germans were about to enter Prague during their occupation of Czechoslovakia Hitler asked Rommel, "What would you do in my place, Colonel?" "I should get into an open car," Rommel said, "and drive through the streets . . . without an escort." The Czech people were by no means pleased by Germany's bloodless conquest of their country, but Hitler took Rommel's advice. Rommel had long respected Hitler, though he disliked his followers, and such acts of personal courage on Hitler's part increased the colonel's admiration for his leader.

With the German invasion of Poland in September, 1939, the Second World War began. It was a spectacular beginning. The Germans demonstrated a new military tactic – the Blitzkrieg (lightning war). The essence of the Blitzkrieg was the armoured spearhead. Panzer (tank) divisions, concentrated on short fronts, cut their way through the defences and penetrated deep into enemy territory. While the panzers cut communications, seized key positions and generally spread confusion in the enemy's rear, the German infantry, following the path the panzers had cut, surrounded and mopped up the enemy at the front. The object of the Blitzkreig was not to destroy the enemy outright nor was it to capture territory and force him to retreat, it was rather to split up and surround the enemy – panic, confusion and lack of supplies would do the rest.

This use of tanks was similar, but on a much larger scale, to the way Rommel had used infantry in the

Italian campaign during the First World War. From Hitler's headquarters Rommel watched and studied the Blitzkrieg offensive which in four weeks completed the conquest of Poland with only small German losses.

With their frontier secure in the east the German Army turned to the west where it faced the belligerent French and British forces. Their plan of attack was to advance into Belgium and draw the enemy forces in Northern France forward to assist the Belgians. This done they would launch a manned tank attack through the Ardennes and drive to the Channel, thereby cutting the enemy forces in two.

Rommel's respect for Hitler had greatly increased during the Polish campaign. "I had great trouble with him," he wrote to his wife, "he was always wanting to be right up with the forward troops. He seemed to enjoy being under fire." Hitler also took a liking to Rommel and upon request gave him the command of the 7th Panzer Division for the forthcoming attack. This division had 218 tanks and, like all panzer divisions, contained artillery, anti-tank guns and motorized infantry.

Above **Rommel (right) with Hitler.**

6. Blitzkrieg in the West

The invasion began on 10th May, 1940. Two days later Rommel's division reached the River Meuse, having met little resistance while passing through the Ardennes. Rommel's infantry had to attempt crossing in rubber boats because the French had blown up the bridges. The crossing took place at Dinant but was soon brought to a stop by the enemy's heavy artillery and rifle fire. From the rocks on the opposite bank the French troops picked off the invaders as they struggled across the river. Some Germans, badly wounded, reached their objective, others drowned. The remainder, shaken by what they had seen, took cover, afraid to expose themselves to the enemy fire.

When Rommel saw what was happening he brought up tanks and artillery and began a fierce bombardment of the French positions. As a result of this the German crossing got under way once again. By nine o'clock next morning they had ferried thirty tanks across the Meuse, and these moved off in the direction of Ouhage.

Rommel had spent much of his time with the forward troops. He had crossed the Meuse in one of the leading tanks. This method of command had many advantages, but it also had its dangers. When nearing their destination the panzers came under heavy artillery and anti-tank fire. Rommel's tank was hit twice – one in the turret and once in the periscope.

Opposite **A picture taken by Rommel of his troops making use of a railway track in France.**

He described what happened next: "The driver promptly opened the throttle and drove straight into the nearest bushes. He had only gone a few yards, however, when the tank slid down a steep slope on the western edge of the wood and finally stopped, canted over on its side, in such a position that the enemy, whose guns were in position about 500 yards away on the edge of the next wood, could not fail to see it. I had been wounded in the right cheek by a small splinter from the shell which had landed in the periscope." He could not bring its gun to bear because his

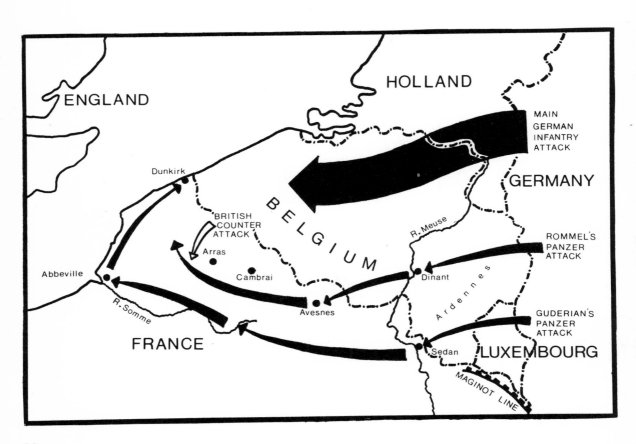

tank was at an angle. Being quite defenceless and an easy target for enemy artillery Rommel and the crew quickly abandoned the tank and had a lucky escape.

Rommel's crossing of the Meuse together with the crossing of General Guderian's panzer divisions further south at Sedan had an alarming effect on the French High Command. The result was that they ordered a retreat to a line fifteen miles behind the Meuse. Rommel's division moved so fast, however, that it reached this line before the retreating French could take up position. With this the French front disintegrated and chaos began to spread throughout the French Army. Thereafter the 7th Panzer Division met only spasmodic opposition, and hundreds of French troops began to surrender.

The Division overcame the French frontier fortifications without serious loss and reached Avesnes on 17th May. By this time the enemy was in a state of complete confusion, a situation which Rommel described as follows: "The French troops were completely overcome by surprise at our sudden appearance, laid down their arms and marched off to the east beside our column. Nowhere was any resistance attempted. Any enemy tanks we met on the road were put out of action as we drove past. The advance went on without a halt to the west. Hundreds upon hundreds of French troops, with their officers, surrendered at our arrival."

By 20th May the 7th Division was past Cambrai and launching an attack in the direction of Arras. The next day, just as Guderian's tanks reached the English Channel and completed the encirclement of the British Expeditionary Force (B.E.F.), the British launched the only significant counter attack of the campaign. With seventy-four tanks the British attacked Rommel's forces south of Arras. Rommel was with his

"The French battery now opened fire on our wood and at any moment we could expect their fire to be aimed at our tank, which was in full view. I therefore decided to abandon it as fast as I could, taking the crew with me. At that moment the subaltern in command of the tanks escorting the infantry reported himself seriously wounded, with the words: 'Herr General, my left arm has been shot off.' We clambered up through the sandy pit, shells crashing and splintering all round." *Erwin Rommel. The Rommel Papers.*

"The people in the houses were rudely awoken by the din of our tanks, the clatter and roar of tracks and engines. Troops lay bivouacked beside the road, military vehicles stood parked in farmyards and in some places on the road itself. Civilians and French troops, their faces distorted with terror, lay huddled in the ditches, alongside hedges and in every hollow beside the road." *Erwin Rommel. The Rommel Papers.*

Above **The Commander of the French IX Corps surrendering personally to Rommel, June, 1940.**

infantry near the village of Wailly when the first British tanks appeared. The German infantry did not stand up to the enemy tanks and began to retreat in confusion. Rommel drove off to a nearby hill where a number of anti-tank and anti-aircraft weapons were in position. More British tanks could then be seen coming towards them from a different direction. Rommel then ran from gun to gun pointing out which tank each was to aim for. A number of British tanks were soon destroyed and the remainder were forced to withdraw. Elsewhere the German artillery and heavy anti-aircraft guns brought the British tank attack to a standstill and inflicted heavy losses. Later a tank versus tank battle flared up when German panzers clashed with British tanks and anti-tank guns. In this both sides sustained approximately equal losses but the British tanks went into retreat – their counter attack was at an end.

After the Arras battle the 7th Division became involved in heavy fighting with the British who were withdrawing towards Dunkirk. During this period Divisional Headquarters came under heavy artillery fire. "I was just making a dash for the signals vehicle," Rommel later wrote, "with Major Erdmann running a few yards in front, when a heavy shell landed close by the house door near which the vehicle was standing. When the smoke cleared Major Erdmann . . . lay face on the ground, dead, his back shattered. I escaped unscathed, though the same shell had wounded several other officers and men." Rommel's good fortune in war was not entirely due to his own abilities – he was also extremely lucky.

The German plan of attack had worked brilliantly, the B.E.F. and French forces in the north had been cut off and, although most of these troops were successfully evacuated from Dunkirk, the French defence now lacked the best part of its Army.

On 5th June, 1940, the second stage of the German campaign began, its object was the defeat of the remaining French forces. Yet again, the Blitzkrieg

"Particularly irate over his sudden disturbance was a French lieutenant-colonel who we overtook with his car jammed in the press of vehicles . . . His eyes glowed with hate and impotent fury and he gave the impression of being a thoroughly fanatical type . . . He was fetched back to Colonel Rothenburg, who signed him to get into his tank. But he curtly refused to come with us, so, after summoning him three times to get in, there was nothing for it but to shoot him."
Erwin Rommel. The Rommel Papers.

35

proved devastating, the French could do little to halt
the German invasion. Rommel's Division crossed the
Somme, cut through the disintegrating French Army
and raced to Cherbourg. At one stage they advanced
150 miles in less than twenty-four hours, which, as one
historian has pointed out, "far exceeded any day's

advance which had ever been made in warfare." On
16th June the demoralized French Government asked
for an armistice. It came into effect on 25th June.

During the offensive in the west the 7th Panzer
Division had captured no less than 97,648 prisoners.
Its losses were only 682 men killed and 296 missing.

Above **A picture taken by Rommel
of his troops storming the
heights beyond the Somme.**

7. Africa: the First Advance

On 10th June, 1940, Benito Mussolini, the dictator of Fascist Italy, brought his country into the war. By that time the B.E.F. had been evacuated from Dunkirk and French resistance had collapsed. A German victory seemed assured – and Mussolini wanted a share of the glory.

In Egypt and the Sudan General Archibald Wavell commanded 50,000 British troops, a force which stood between the vast Italian armies (some half a million men) in Libya and Italian East Africa. It seemed as though nothing could prevent an Italian conquest of Egypt. But the Italian Army was badly equipped and badly led. Their offensive was slow to get off the ground, and it was not until September, 1940, that the Italians in Libya moved into Egypt. They went only fifty miles through an undefended area, then stopped to establish fortifications.

By December the British forces had been reinforced and the Italians had advanced no further. Wavell therefore launched an attack. The Italian Army crumbled before the British forces and the battle soon developed into a race – the Italians abandoning their weapons and fleeing to the west and the British chasing after them. After chasing them across Cyrenaica the British cut off the retreating Italians near Beda Fomm. With that the British had captured the greater part of

Opposite **German infantry encircling Mersa Brega in Cyrenaica.**

39

Above **A map showing the campaign area of North Africa.**

> "We were twice attacked by British ground-strafing aircraft about ten miles west of Bardia. Corporal Eggert, the driver of my cross-country vehicle, was killed; the vehicle received 25 hits. My dispatch rider, Private Kanthak, was also killed. The driver of the Mammoth [Rommel's command vehicle] was wounded by a bullet which came through the visor. Leaving Berndt with the damaged vehicles, I climbed into the driving seat of my Mammoth and drove myself." *Erwin Rommel. The Rommel Papers.*

the Italian Army in North Africa. According to Rommel, "All that remained of it was a few lorry columns and hordes of unarmed soldiers in full flight to the west."

Hitler decided to support his floundering Italian allies by sending two German divisions to North Africa. This force – the Africa Corps – was placed under Rommel's command. The first part of the Africa Corps arrived in mid-February, 1941, by which time the British had reached El Agheila. In order to stem the British advance Rommel sent his German troops up to the front immediately. To deceive the British he had a number of dummy tanks made and mounted on Volkswagen motor cars. From a distance and from the air these made his forces appear much stronger than they really were. However, the British had already come to a stop because a large part of their North

African Army had been withdrawn and sent to Greece.

As the British were not moving forward Rommel began a local attack of his own. The weak British forces at El Agheila soon withdrew and the Africa Corps followed up with a successful attack on the stronger British positions at Mersa Brega. After this Rommel decided to press forward with the small forces he then had available: "Luftwaffe (airforce) reports clearly showed that the enemy was tending to draw back and this was confirmed by reconnaissance patrols... It was a chance I could not resist and I gave orders for Agedabia to be attacked and taken, in spite of the fact that our instructions were not to undertake any such operations before the end of May." His two divisions were arriving bit by bit, the complete force was not expected before the end of May. "The effect of this audacious thrust was magical," says historian

Above **Only seven weeks after reaching North Africa Rommel captured a large British force, including three generals. He is seen here (extreme left) talking to Major-General Richard Gambier-Parry (extreme right).**

"Probably never before in modern warfare had such a completely unprepared offensive as this raid through Cyrenaica been attempted.
"... The British had been completely deceived as to our real strength. Their moves would have been very astute, if they had been attacked by a force as strong as they supposed." *Erwin Rommel. The Rommel Papers.*

B. H. Liddell Hart, "the British forces hastily fell back in confusion . . ."

Rommel kept the Africa Corps hard on the heels of the retreating enemy. Within two weeks he had driven the British out of Cyrenaica and back to Egypt. However, the British held on to Tobruk with its Italian built defences, and, with their command of the sea, they were in a position to keep the garrison well supplied.

Rommel now found to his cost that the British who had been routed in the open desert were very difficult to dislodge from fixed positions. He mounted two large scale attacks on Fortress Tobruk, but both were unsuccessful. The Africa Corps suffered heavy losses in the attempt to batter a way through the minefields and past the bunkers tenaciously defended by Australian troops. And Rommel himself came near to death when his command vehicle was strafed by a British plane. With his forces depleted and the hostile Tobruk garrison in his rear Rommel's advance was brought to a stop and the front line established near Sollum.

"The enemy fought with remarkable tenacity. Even their wounded went on defending themselves with small arms fire and stayed in the fight to their last breath.

". . . Shortly afterwards a batch of some fifty or sixty Australian prisoners were marched off close besides us – immensely big and powerful men, who without question represented an élite formation of the British Empire, a fact that was also evident in battle." *Erwin Rommel. The Rommel Papers.*

Opposite **British troops manning an A.A. gun outside Tobruk, 1941.**

8. The Desert Fox

After his hectic advance to the Egyptian frontier Rommel went over to the defensive in order to give the Africa Corps time to reorganize and build up strength for the next battle. The nature of war in the desert was now becoming apparent; it was a war of rapid advances and counter attacks followed by periods of relative calm. During these periods of calm Rommel and his desert soldiers could settle down to a fairly normal routine.

After his evening meal Rommel would listen to the news on the radio before attending to his correspondence and official papers. He used to write to his wife every day unless he was particularly busy, and he also kept up a correspondence with the men of his First World War battalion. If he found time for reading he chose either a newspaper or a book on a military subject. Rommel always rose early in the morning and on an average day would set out at 7 a.m. to visit the front line. Travelling in an open car, he usually went far beyond his own front line positions – out into "no man's land." There he would observe his own army's defensive positions from the direction that the enemy saw them.

If, while scanning the land through his field glasses, he saw a badly camouflaged position or something else which displeased him, he would immediately drive back

"When an attack is ordered, the men must never get the feeling that their casualties have been calculated in advance according to the laws of probability, for that is the end of all enthusiasm. The soldier must continually receive fresh justification for his confidence, otherwise it is soon lost. He must go into battle easy in mind and with no doubt about the command under which he is fighting." *Erwin Rommel. The Rommel Papers.*

Opposite **Rommel and Aide (Bayerlein).**

45

Below **Rommel standing outside his sparsely furnished tent.**

and deliver a personal reprimand to the officer in charge. Although he was very popular with the men of the Africa Corps he was not particularly amicable towards his subordinates; "It's a great thing to be a Field Marshal," he once said, "and still remember how to talk to them like a sergeant-major."

Rommel would not tolerate anything second rate, he expected the best from his men and he usually got it. Any unsatisfactory officer was soon replaced. It did not

take the soldiers of the Africa Corps long to realize that Rommel was a man they could trust. He was not a shadowy figure sitting at a desk far behind the front line, but a man who might turn up anywhere at anytime, a man who would never rely on the reports of a subordinate when he could look into things himself. In this way he always knew what the real condition of his army was, and, just as important, his men knew that he understood their problems. Rommel's attitude towards military leadership is best illustrated by his own words: "The commander must try, above all, to establish personal and comradely contact with his men, but without giving away an inch of his authority."

During a battle Rommel was always active in the forward areas – travelling in one of the leading tanks or dashing from place to place making sure that his troops were doing their job properly. So great was his concern with speed that he could never get his mobile troops to move fast enough. His personal reconaissance aircraft, which he sometimes piloted himself, was of great assistance to the fast moving Desert Fox. This small, light plane was not dependant upon airfields, but could land almost anywhere in flat desert areas. In this, Rommel made a habit of dropping out of the sky to hurry along a slow column or give fresh instructions to his officers.

This method of command was somewhat unconventional, as Liddle Hart explains: "Rommel has been much criticized by more orthodox soldiers, German as well as British, for the frequency with which he was away from his headquarters and his fondness for taking direct control of the fight. But that direct control, although it caused some of his troubles, was the prime cause of his great successes." Rommel believed that war in the desert was like war at sea.

"... the struggle in the desert is best compared with a battle at sea. Whoever has the weapons with the greatest range has the longest arm, exactly as at sea. Whoever has the greater mobility, through efficient motorization and efficient line of supply, can by swift action compel his opponent to act according to his wishes." *Erwin Rommel, quoted in H. W. Schmidt's With Rommel in the Desert.*

Above **Rommel in his aircraft.**

Just as a naval commander could not conduct a battle from a shore base, so a desert commander could not conduct a battle from a headquarters hundreds of miles behind the front.

Although he was primarily a fighting general, Rommel did not fail to give some thought to grand strategy. It was a great disappointment to him that the German High Command did not understand the importance of the war in North Africa. He was told "that the Army High Command regarded the North African theatre as a lost cause and that they were setting the German troops no other task but to delay the collapse of Italian resistance in Libya for as long as possible." Rommel realized that if he could defeat the British forces in Egypt he could not only cut the Suez Canal, and thereby close the Eastern Mediterranean to enemy shipping, but also move into Persia and Iraq almost unopposed.

Persia and Iraq were of key importance. The oilfields of these countries could have supplied the Axis Powers (Germay and Italy) with the petrol they badly needed for their war effort. An Axis occupation of Persia and Iraq would also prevent the Americans from sending vast quantities of war matériel to the Russians through the Persian Gulf.

To add to Rommel's difficulties, the command structure in Africa was very complicated and the German's relationship with the Italian Supreme Command was a bitter one. Rommel had Italian troops under his command as well as the Africa Corps, and, although ultimately responsible only to Hitler, he was nominally under the command of the Italian General Bastico and the Italian Supreme Command.

"Bombastico" was Rommel's nickname for General Bastico; as the name suggests Rommel did not have much respect for him. He felt the same about the other Italian generals, too. Field Marshal Kesselring noted: "Rommel was unwilling to budge an inch to avoid treading on the corns of the susceptible Italians." Rommel's main problem with the Italians was that they handled his army's supplies. In 1942, when the British began to sink large numbers of Italian ships, Rommel's supply problem became a nightmare. The supplies he received were only a fraction of what the Italians had promised him. Rommel greatly resented this, believing that the supply problem could have been solved had it not been for the incompetence of the Italian Command.

"In battle Rommel was at his best. He was a natural leader and he relied, both instinctively and deliberately, upon personal leadership . . . the secret of his early successes was that he did not have to wait for information to be filtered back to him through the usual channels of command. He was up to see for himself, in his aircraft, his tank, his armoured car, his Volkswagen, or on foot." *Desmond Young. Rommel.*

Overleaf A picture taken by Rommel of an Italian gun crew.

9. The Desert War

"At the time we believed that the Africa Corps was a *corps d'élite*, hand-picked from volunteers and specially toughened and trained for desert warfare." This impression of a British officer serving in the desert at the time was far from true. The Africa Corps consisted of ordinary units of the German Army. They were not volunteers nor were they specially selected or given any special training to fight in the desert. Like most German soldiers they were tough, well equipped, and well trained in the art of war. What made the Africa Corps different was mainly due to their leader.

The Africa Corps was, except for a few short periods here and there, under Rommel's command from beginning to end. They were a relatively small army far from home – only a few of them had been outside Europe before, so to most the desert was an alien world. This gave Rommel an exceptional opportunity to impress his personality on his troops, and few commanders have ever made such a good impression as Rommel. It was largely thanks to him that the Africa Corps maintained the exceptionaly high morale, pride and determination which characterized it.

Together the Africa Corps and Italian forces formed the Panzer Group Africa, later called the Panzer Army Africa. In any comparison between the Africa Corps and its Italian comrades, the Italians come off badly.

Opposite **A German gun crew in action in the Western Desert.**

53

Below **Rommel with two senior Italian officers.**

Of course, every army contains both good and bad soldiers, but what made the Italian Army exceptional was that it seemed to have contained a higher proportion of bad soldiers than any other army involved in the war. The quality of its equipment, too, left much to be desired. According to Rommel the Italian Army "was designed for a colonial war against insurgent tribesmen . . . Its tanks and armoured vehicles were

too light and their engines under-powered . . . Most of the guns with which the artillery was equipped dated from the 1914–18 war and had a short range . . . But its worst feature was the fact that a great part of the Italian Army consisted of non-motorized infantry. In the North African desert non-motorized troops are of practically no value against a motorized enemy . . ."

The British forces in North Africa, named the Eighth Army in September, 1941, consisted of Australian, New Zealander, South African and Indian as well as British troops. It was a fully motorized and well-equipped army; although the Africa Corps had better equipment at the beginning of the desert war the Eighth Army gained this advantage towards the end. British tactics, however, were not as advanced as those of the Germans. They often committed their tanks in "penny packets," while Rommel, using his tanks in mass, could overwhelm these small groups one at a time. The morale of the British troops was usually high, and they proved tenacious in defence, if un-enterprising in attack.

In their fight against the Panzer Group the British generals were faced with an unusual problem – Rommel's popularity with their own troops. It is not unusual for soldiers to respect their enemy, but the troops of the Eighth Army had something near affection for Rommel. In the hope of remedying the situation the Commander-in-Chief Middle East, General Auchinleck, sent out an order to his officers instructing them to talk of "the Germans" or "the enemy . . . and not always keep harping on Rommel."

For the Germans, Italians and British alike living conditions in the desert were far from pleasant. In letters to his wife and son Rommel spoke of the atrocious heat of both day and night: "One lies in bed, tossing and turning and dripping with sweat," and of sand

"There exists a real danger that our friend Rommel is becoming a kind of magician or bogey-man to our troops, who are talking far too much about him. He is by no means a superman, although he is undoubtedly very energetic and able. Even if he were a superman it would still be highly undesirable that our men should credit him with supernatural powers." *Part of General Auchinleck's order.*

storms "so thick you could only see two to three yards." He was particularly lucid on the subject of insects, besides the mosquitos and "endless swarms of flies" he was also troubled by parasites: "My bed is standing on tins filled with water and I hope the night will be a little more restful from now on. Some of the others are having a bad time with fleas." Later he overcame the problem: "I've been free of bugs ever since I had petrol poured over my iron bedstead, and set light to. They must have been in the framework." The Africa Corps was supplied with very poor rations, yet Rommel, unlike most other senior officers, chose to eat the same rations as his men, except on those rare occasions when his cook was provided with fresh venison.

Rommel had always liked hunting and during the time his headquarters were at Gazala he was able to enjoy this sport in the nearby gazelle country. Rommel was as determined in the hunt as he was in war. Heinz Schmidt, then an officer on Rommel's staff, has left us this description of what happened when Rommel was once chasing after a gazelle in his car: "The ground was pitted with fox-holes. It grew even more rugged. The mad temper of the chase became a danger to life and limb. What if Germany's top general in Africa broke his neck in a senseless pursuit of a buck?

"The chase went on. It looked as though the game would escape. The ground got rougher and rougher. But Rommel grew more and more determined, and kept urging his driver to step on the gas." He finally caught up with the gazelle, shot it with his pistol and was able to supplement the inadequate rations with a hunk of fresh meat."

The formidable leader of the Panzer Army was not always the hunter. Sometimes he was the target. The British made a number of attempts to kill him. On one

"... it was Rommel who, almost at once, by personal influence and example, by force of character, by taking more risks than his troops, converted [the Afrika Korps] into that tough, truculent, resilient fighting force we knew. Rommel *was* the Afrika Korps, to his own men as well as to the enemy. It was he who made them bold, self-confident and even arrogant in battle. It was he who taught them to pull the last ounce out of themselves and never to admit that they were beaten." *Desmond Young. Rommel.*

occasion twenty-seven commandos landed behind German lines, raided a house which they thought to be Rommel's headquarters and killed the four German occupants. In fact the house was not Rommel's headquarters, and anyway the Desert Fox was in Rome at the time.

One of the most miserable aspects of desert life was the frequency with which the soldiers were afflicted with sickness and disease. The naturally harsh conditions, combined with the poor rations, gave rise to jaundice, dysentry and scurvy. The Germans, being totally unaccustomed to the desert, suffered most of all, and the Africa Corps was decimated by disease. Rommel himself fell victim to a number of ailments, and he was a sick man for much of his time in North Africa.

In a war that brought unprecedented destruction and loss of civilian life it is surprising to find that the desert war was conducted honourably. Rommel was concerned to see that the war was fought according to the rules. He was furious when he heard reports that on one occasion British troops had bayoneted German wounded. Fortunately incidents of this kind were extremely rare in North Africa as the British also had a great respect for the rules of war. The matter was complicated in October, 1942, when Hitler issued an order which stated that all Allied commandos should "be slaughtered to the last man," even if they had surrendered. Rommel had always believed that an officer should obey his superiors, but he did not obey, nor did he ever intend to obey, these instructions. When he received a copy of the order he immediately burnt it. Desmond Young, who served with the Eighth Army until he was captured by the enemy, said of the Africa Corps: " . . . after the first rough pounce, it treated [its prisoners] with almost old-world courtesy."

"To us this survival of chivalry came as a surprise. Knowing nothing of the feud between the Party and the Wehrmacht, of the Nazis' jealousy of the Army, of the contempt of the officer class for the 'brown scum,' of the long, if weak-kneed, opposition of many Generals to their Fuehrer, we naturally lumped all Germans together." *Desmond Young. Rommel.*

"**The simple life here suits me
better than the fleshpots of
France.**" *Extract from one of Rommel's
letters to his wife.*

59

10. The Battle of Gazala

The British resumed the offensive after Rommel had been stopped in April, 1941. In midsummer they launched an attack against his defensive positions – "Operation Battleaxe" – but this proved a costly failure. A second attack, codenamed "Operation Crusader," began in November. The Eighth Army had a two to one advantage in tanks and planes over the Panzer group. After heavy fighting with great losses on both sides Rommel was driven back to Mersa Brega. But, within a few weeks, Rommel turned the tide yet again and drove the British back 250 miles to Gazala. Then, while the Eighth Army was preparing for the next offensive, he struck again.

The British defensive line at Gazala consisted of a long minefield stretching from the coast out into the desert. This linked a number of strong points, known as boxes, which had the protection of surrounding minefields and barbed wire. The Eighth Army's tanks were kept further back ready for a counter attack. The Battle of Gazala began when the Panzer Army attacked this line on 26th May, 1942.

Against the 100,000 soldiers of the Eighth Army Rommel had 90,000, mostly Italians. The Eighth Army also had a superiority in tanks – 850 against Rommel's 560. However the Panzer Army may have been supported by a greater number of aircraft – the

Opposite **Rommel preparing his Egyptian attack with General Nehring.**

records differ on this point.

Rommel divided his army into two parts. In the north and centre of the Gazala line the unmotorized Italian infantry made faint attacks to distract the enemy. Meanwhile the Africa Corps and the motorized Italian forces made the main attack. During the night Rommel led the 10,000 vehicles of his striking force down into the desert. They swept round the southern extremity of the Gazala line then went up into the enemy's rear.

It was Rommel's intention to push north until he reached the Mediterranean Sea, but his plans were thwarted when his forces clashed with the enemy's tanks: "There was . . . a British surprise awaiting us here, one which was not to our advantage – the new Grant tank which was used in this battle for the first time on African soil. Tank after tank, German and British, was shattered in the fire of the tank-guns." The quality of the Africa Corps' tanks had previously been superior to those of the British. Now the Eighth Army had 167 of the American-made General Grant tanks each of which was armed with a 75mm gun; the German Panzer Mark IV had similar armament but the Africa Corps had only forty of these.

The new British tanks had their effect. After a day of confused fighting Rommel had lost a third of his tanks. Indecisive fighting continued on the second day, leaving Rommel with only 240 tanks with which to face the remaining 420 British tanks.

Rommel, now really in trouble, took up a defensive position in an area known as "the Cauldron." Not only was he faced by numerically superior British tanks, but in his rear he had a British minefield, guarded by the 150th Brigade's box. His forces had been unable to cut a path through the minefield as planned and he was therefore becoming short of supplies. But, just as

> "I held my fire, but the companies on the right let rip with the 50mm 'pak' guns. I saw some of the shells bounce harmlessly off the Grants. On the other hand the enemy's replying fire was grim. His shellbursts among our infantry were particularly deadly.
> "Now a shiver went through me. From out of the dip emerged rank after rank of the new tanks – a good sixty in all. They came at us with every muzzle blazing."
> *Heinz Schmidt. With Rommel in the Desert.*

Rommel expected, the British did not take advantage of his weak position. They made a number of piecemeal attacks which the Panzer Army beat off by skilful use of anti-tank guns. Meanwhile the Panzer Army overwhelmed the 150th Brigade's box and cleared a path for supplies. By 6th June the British attacks had reduced their tank strength to 170, and the Panzer Army was firmly astride the Gazala line. The British had missed their chance. As Rommel put it: "In a moment so decisive they should have thrown in all the strength they could muster. What is the use of having overall superiority if one allows one's formation to be smashed piece by piece by an enemy who, in each separate action, is able to concentrate superior strength at the decisive point?"

To the south the Free French still held the box at Bir Hacheim. This was Rommel's next target, and after a tough fight it was captured. Having cleared the southern part of the Gazala line he struck eastward on June 11th. By this time the Eighth Army had received reinforcements which brought their tank strength up to 330. However, in a three day battle the German tactics proved superior. Most of the British tanks were destroyed and Rommel gained a numerical superiority of this essential weapon for the first time. He had clearly won the battle, and the British knew it. In the northern half of the line they began a hasty retreat to prevent themselves being cut off.

Rommel exploited the Eighth Army's defeat brilliantly. The main part of the British force was retreating to the Egyptian border while another part began occupying the defences of Tobruk. Hot on the heels of the retreating enemy, Rommel launched an attack on Tobruk before the defence could be properly organized. This was a tactic he had used during the First World War – and it was just as effective in 1942.

"Looking back on the first day's fighting, it was clear that our plan to overrun the British forces behind the Gazala line had not succeeded. The advance to the coast had also failed . . . The principle cause was our underestimation of the strength of the British armoured divisions. The advent of the new American tank had torn great holes in our ranks. Our entire force now stood in heavy and destructive combat with a superior enemy." *Erwin Rommel. The Rommel Papers.*

Right **Rommel with some of his men pictured shortly before the fall of Tobruk.**

On 20th June the Panzer Army broke through the Tobruk defences and entered the city. The garrison of 35,000 men surrendered the following day. Rommel had been unable to capture Tobruk during an eight month seige the year before, now it fell to him in one day.

The Desert Fox was at the height of success. Two days after the fall of Tobruk he was given the rank of Field Marshal – a unusual honour in view of the fact that in the German Army promotion normally came with seniority. Rommel, aged forty-nine, was Germany's youngest Field Marshal.

> "Tobruk was one of the strongest fortresses in North Africa. In 1941, with magnificent troops in its garrison, it had presented us with immense difficulties. Many attacks had collapsed in its defences and much of its outer perimeter had literally been soaked in blood. Often the battle had raged round a square yard at a time. We were no strangers to Tobruk.
> "To every man of us, Tobruk was a symbol of British resistance and we were now going to finish with it for good."
> *Erwin Rommel. The Rommel Papers.*

11. Alamein

The Panzer Army reached the Alamein line on 30th June, 1942. This line of minefields and boxes was the Eighth Army's last defensive position in Egypt – the one obstacle that stood between Rommel and the conquest of Alexandria and Cairo.

The fighting at Gazala and Tobruk had not failed to leave its mark on the Panzer Army. Rommel had few serviceable tanks left and his troops were exhausted, but, nonetheless, he immediately mounted an attack on the Alamein position. He seems to have understood that this chance would not come again and that he was closer to complete victory than he had ever been before or would ever be again. But, after three days fighting, victory was denied him and he was forced to break off the attack. His overstrained soldiers were badly in need of a rest and they were also becoming short of supplies, being so far away from their bases.

On 21st July the reinforced Eighth Army went over to the offensive with a superior number of tanks. Rommel was extremely worried by this attack, but he finally beat the British off by his skilful defensive tactics.

Although the Eighth Army suffered heavy losses, they had put an end to Rommel's advance. During August a lull settled over the battlefield as both sides began to build up strength and reorganize. Auchinleck was replaced as Commander-in-Chief Middle East by

Opposite **German prisoners taken during the first two days fighting at El Alamein waiting to be transported to prisoner-of-war camps.**

General Alexander, and General Montgomery took over command of the Eighth Army. Rommel, however, was impatient to begin the next battle. He was aware that the Eighth Army was receiving reinforcements at a far greater rate than his own forces. He therefore decided to force the issue before the enemy built up an overwhelming superiority.

On 30th August the Panzer Army began a full scale assault on the Alamein line. This, the Battle of Alam Halfa, was to be Rommel's last attempt to destroy the Eighth Army and conquer Egypt. It was a dismal failure. The attack made slow progress against the Eighth Army's superior numbers and sound defence. After Rommel's forces broke through the line they found themselves immobilized by a shortage of petrol. While exposed in the open desert the Africa Corps was repeatedly attacked by R.A.F. bombers which caused severe losses of both men and matériel. Three days later the Africa Corps was forced to withdraw. It was a fore-taste of battles to come.

The final Battle of Alamein, and the one which is remembered by that name, was, as Rommel described it, a "battle without a hope." Rommel had about 50,000 German troops and 54,000 Italians with which to face the 195,000 men of the Eighth Army. And he had less than 500 tanks while the British had more than twice that number. The Eighth Army was also superior in artillery, having approximately a two to one advantage in field guns and anti-tank guns. The Allies were stronger in the air and had the most powerful bomber force yet seen in North Africa.

As we have seen, Rommel has been outnumbered before and had still been victorious – but this time his army was at a great qualitative disadvantage. Half of his tanks were Italian, of obsolete design and little use against the British tanks, over four-hundred of which were American-built Sherman and Grant tanks.

Another crucial factor against Rommel was the shortage of supplies. British air and naval action had begun to have a devastating effect on supply ships crossing the Mediterranean. In October half of Rommel's supplies were lost before they could reach Africa. As a result the Germans were very low on artillery ammunition, and there was a shortage of petrol, which limited the mobility of Rommel's forces – an enormous disadvantage in desert warfare. The German rations – which were never good – deteriorated even further because of the shortages, causing a severe outbreak of sickness among the men of the Africa Corps. Before the British offensive many key German officers had been forced to leave Africa due to sickness. Rommel was one of them.

Prior to the Battle of Alam Halfa Rommel's medical adviser had sent a message to the German High Command which said, "Field Marshal Rommel suffering from chronic stomach and intestinal catarrh, nasal diptheria and considerable circulation trouble. He is not in a fit condition to command the forthcoming offensive." Nevertheless, Rommel had remained in command for the battle and did not return to Europe for treatment until 23rd September. He was replaced by General Stumme.

The British offensive began on 23rd October; the following day the unfortunate General Stumme fell from his car and died of a heart attack. Hitler immediately asked Rommel to resume command, which he did despite the fact that he had not yet fully recovered. He arrived back on 25th October to take charge of a defence which had by then been deeply dented and had lost almost half its effective tanks that day in unsuccessful counter attacks.

> "I knew that the fall of Tobruk and the collapse of the Eighth Army was the one moment in the African war when the road to Alexandria lay open and virtually undefended . . . If success had depended, as in times gone by, on the strength of will of my men and their officers, then we would have overrun Alamein. But our sources of supply had dried up – thanks to the idleness and muddle of the supply authorities on the mainland." *Erwin Rommel. The Rommel Papers.*

Rommel's defences lay behind a thick minefield running from the coast to the Qattara Depression (an impassable region of salt marsh and soft sand). His Panzers were deployed, ready for a quick counter attack should the minefield be breached.

Montgomery's attack came at night. After an artillery bombardment from over one thousand guns

the Eighth Army's infantry advanced through the darkness. At first the Panzer Army held back the enemy and the British losses began to mount. Hundreds of British tanks were destroyed as they battered their way through Rommel's defences – for every German tank destroyed the British lost three. But the Eighth Army could afford this disproportional loss. The Africa Corps was slowly worn down until it had only a handful of panzers left to fight the masses of British tanks still on the battlefield.

Even so the Panzer Army still kept the British in check with a screen of anti-tank guns and more and more British tanks were put out of action as they tried to smash a way through. However, Montgomery remained determined. He continued the attack.

By 3rd November the Panzer Army was at the end of its strength. Rommel was forced to begin a withdrawal towards Fuka. As the withdrawal was getting under way, an order arrived from Hitler. It exorted Rommel to lead his men to "victory or death," and instructed him to "yield not a yard of ground." The order was insane, but Rommel felt bound to obey it. He did so with great reluctance.

The next morning the British broke through. Finally, in the afternoon, Rommel got Hitler's permission to retreat. The delay might have cost Germany the entire Panzer Army had the British not been so slow to exploit the situation. As it was, although many were captured, Rommel's forces were able to fall back and begin their eleventh hour retreat.

Above **Rommel (right) receiving first reports of the Battle of Alamein.**

Opposite **British infantry charge an enemy position at El Alamein.**

12. Defeat in Africa

Four days after the Eighth Army's breakthrough at Alamein a huge armada landed a second Allied force in French North Africa. This Anglo–American force began an eastward advance into Tunisia. To Rommel's army, which was retreating westwards with the Eighth Army following up behind, this looked extremely menacing. In the event, however, the Allied advance into Tunisia was stopped by German forces quickly rushed over from Europe.

But there was no help for Rommel, who was beginning a long struggle to keep his army from destruction. "Vehicle columns, their lorries full of stragglers, jammed up and choked the whole road, while overhead the R.A.F. reigned supreme, flying one attack after the other against every worthwhile target."

Rommel knew that his forces were too weak to stand their ground. Not only had most of his troops been captured at Alamein, but most of those that had escaped had lost their weapons. When his retreating columns reach Sollum his fighting strength was down to 5,000 Germans, 2,500 Italians and 21 tanks. There was nothing for it but to continue the retreat: "It was obvious that with these forces we could not afford to await an attack by hundreds of British tanks and several motorized infantry divisions." Without reinforcements or re-equipment the Panzer Army did not stand a

Opposite **Axis prisoners taken during the Allied offensive against Rommel.**

chance of holding off the Eighth Army in the open desert. Rommel therefore decided that unless he received reinforcements he would withdraw all the way back to Tunisia, where a strong defensive position was available and where he would be able to link up with the other German forces.

But the Panzer Army did not obtain the reinforcements and equipment it so badly needed. In fact Rommel was hard put to find even the petrol necessary to keep his army on the move because the supply situation had become so bad. Yet his retreat was skilfully executed. Whenever a defensive position was available his forces would occupy it. Then the Eighth Army would stop and prepare for an attack, but before the preparations were completed Rommel would slip away to his next defensive position. These tactics gained time, and by keeping his army together prevented his retreat from turning into a rout. It was, therefore, not a continuous retreat but a series of withdrawals and stops.

The enemy was not Rommel's only problem – he also had trouble with his superiors. Orders from Hitler of the sort he issued during the Battle of Alamein – instructing Rommel to hold his position and fight to the last man – would occasionally come through. Mussolini also sent similar instructions. This interference was a thorn in Rommel's side, although he usually managed to get his own way in the end.

To Rommel the situation was quite simple. On one occasion when told to hold his position "at all costs" he explained, "We either lose the position four days earlier and save the army, or lose both position and army four days later."

Three months after the defeat at Alamein the Panzer Army moved into Tunisia. The retreat of 1,200 miles was over. Rommel hoped that eventually he would be able to evacuate his troops from Africa and use them for the defence of Europe. He had been tremendously impressed by the output of armaments from the U.S.A., and because of this he believed that the Axis forces were no longer capable of achieving ultimate victory in Africa.

In the meantime, with the two Axis armies linked up, Rommel saw a chance to strike a blow at the Americans. The result was the Battle of Kasserine, which came as a considerable shock to the untried American soldiers. However Rommel was not given the freedom of action necessary to exploit the initial success and the offensive was brought to a stop. Had his superiors not interfered the Allies might have suffered a disastrous setback.

After the failure of this offensive Rommel realized that the Italian and German forces would be destroyed if they stayed in Africa much longer. On 7th March, 1943, he returned to Europe with the intention of persuading Hitler and Mussolini to evacuate the troops in Africa. His efforts proved fruitless. Not only did Hitler refuse evacuation from Africa, he even had hopes of resuming the offensive. Rommel was subsequently relieved of his command and instructed to take his long-deferred sick leave.

As it happened, the events in Africa followed Rommel's expectations. The Allies pushed back the Axis forces until they were finally overrun. By 13th May, it was all over. What was left of Rommel's faithful Africa Corps was marched away into prisoner of war camps.

But for their leader there remained another battle to fight.

> "... magnificent and entirely spontaneous loyalty between officers and men kept alive even through the darkest hours of the African war. Even in Tunis, the troops retained full confidence in their command– probably a unique phenomenon after a retreat of 1,200 miles. But a bitter fate denied them any escape to Europe. I have evidence that in captivity my men have borne their lot with the same spirit of loyalty that distinguished the Panzer Army during two years of African war.
> *Erwin Rommel. The Rommel Papers.*

Above **Africa Corps prisoners being transported to prisoner-of-war camps.**

13. The Atlantic Wall

After the evacuation of the B.E.F. from Dunkirk the British had begun building coastal defences to repel the expected German invasion. Now, in 1944, the situation was reversed. The British, spurred on by their victories in North Africa and Italy, prepared to invade the German Empire in northern Europe. Now it was Germany's turn to construct a coastal defence system – "The Atlantic Wall."

With their air and sea superiority the British could in theory strike anywhere from Norway to the French border with Spain, but a large scale invasion could not in fact be effected so far from the English coast. The Germans therefore rightly assumed that the Allies would land on the coast of northern France, Belgium or the Netherlands. At the beginning of 1944 Rommel took command of the troops in this threatened area.

He soon discovered that the defences were in no state to repel an invasion. Field Marshal von Rundstedt, then Commander-in-Chief West and Rommel's immediate superior, described the Atlantic Wall as a "Propaganda Wall." By this he meant that although it had been given a good deal of publicity and proclaimed a formidable defence, in reality it did not amount to much.

There was a difference of opinion between Rundstedt and Rommel as to how the coming battle should be

Opposite **Rommel (left) inspecting coastal defences in Europe.**

> "... I therefore consider that an attempt must be made, using every possible expedient, to beat off the enemy landings on the coast and to fight the battle in the more or less strongly fortified coastal strips. This will require the contruction of a fortified and mined zone extending from the coast some five miles or six miles inland and defended both to the sea and to the land. The existing minefields, fenced in with wire, present little or no obstacle and wide lanes would be cleared through them in a very short while." *Erwin Rommel. The Rommel Papers.*

fought. Having so few troops to defend such a long coastline and not knowing where the Allies would attack, Rundstedt wanted to keep the best part of his army and particularly the panzer division well back from the coast. His plan was to wait until the Allies landed and then launch a powerful counter attack with concentrated forces. In this way he hoped to bring a greater part of his army into battle than he would be able to do if he spread his entire force thinly along the coast.

Rommel by contrast planned to destroy the enemy on the beaches, and for this he wanted his forces either on the coast or nearby, ready for an immediate small scale counter attack. He believed that with their tremendous air superiority the Allies would be able to keep the German forces pinned down and prevent the troop movements necessary for a large scale counter offensive. He was convinced that if the Allies were given sufficient time to build up reinforcements after they landed the battle would be lost. In the event, however, neither Rommel nor Rundstedt could put their plans into operation.

In the six months prior to the invasion Rommel did much to strengthen the coastal defences. He had thou-

Right **Rommel (left) inspecting tanks in France, 1944.**

78

sands of obstacles placed on the beaches to impede landing craft and hinder enemy infantry as they struggled ashore. For this purpose he used anti-tank obtsacles and stakes driven into the sand at low tide. Some of these obstacles had steel cutters to rip open the bottoms of enemy boats, others were topped with mines. Rommel used a variety of mines both on the beaches and in extensive minefields inland. In threatened areas he had tree trunks set up like telegraph poles to prevent enemy gliders landing. These were capped with explosive and wired together so that when a glider crashed into the wire the explosives were detonated. To draw enemy fire Rommel had dummy gun batteries and dummy trenches constructed while his real batteries and trenches were camouflaged. Dummy minefields were also added to confuse the enemy.

What Rommel achieved was largely a result of his own imaginative improvization, but his achievements fell far short of his plans. He was made powerless by shortages – shortages of mines, shortages of concrete for bomb proof shelters, shortages of steel for beach obstacles and gun cupolas, and shortages of manpower.

In 1939 the Germans had built the "Seigfried Line," a fortified line along their border with France. A small force garrisoning this line prevented a French invasion while the main part of the German Army attacked Poland. In 1944 the Germans were not so fortunate. Rommel had not enough matériel to make up for his shortages of troops. Neither were his troops of first rate quality. Whilst waiting for the invasion many of the men had become lethargic while other units had been sent to France merely to recuperate from a spell on the Russian front. Once again Rommel had a great effect even upon these dispirited men. As one commentator put it: "He changed the atmosphere of despondancy and vague hope to one of hard work and clear plans."

"Rommel could not get enough mines and demanded millions to lay in extensive fields. As he could not obtain them in sufficient numbers from Germany he set French factories to work.
"His vivid imagnination was always furnishing him with new ideas. Thus he wanted these minefields to be concealed under brambles, and the most cunnnig contraptions suggested themselves to him whereby sham minefields were to be laid by way of deception." *Gunther Blumentritt. Von Rundstedt, the Soldier and the Man.*

"Rommel's brain worked incessantly on new ideas. No landscape, no historic building interested him; he was just a soldier. During a meal he would often take his pencil and a sheet of paper and sketch some new technical idea. Then he would hand it to his engineer general with the request that he would give his views on it next morning before starting out." *Gunther Blumentritt. Von Rundstedt, the Soldier and the Man.*

14. The Last Battle

It was clear to Rommel that if the Allies could gain a bridgehead sufficiently wide and deep to build up their strength on the northern coast of Europe, then the invasion would be irresistable. As the Allies' total resources were so much greater than the Germans,' Rommel was determined not to give them enough space to pile up their massed power in France. In his view the first twenty-four hours would be crucial. None of this, however, was clear to either Rundstedt or Hitler.

Montgomery was in command of the Allied invasion force and, as at Alamein, he was backed by overwhelming air power. Before the invasion the R.A.F. bombed Rommel's defences and destroyed bridges to hamper German troop movements.

In the early morning of 6th June, 1944, a vast armada appeared off the coast of Normandy – the Allied invasion, "Overlord," had begun. It opened with a cannonade as the battleships used their huge guns to shatter the beach defences. Next came the landing craft and special floating tanks. They landed at half tide, thereby avoiding Rommel's obstacles which were positioned to obstruct a landing at high tide. Fire from the special tanks gave cover to the infantry as they crossed the beaches and took up positions inland.

The D-day landings were made on five beaches by British, American and Canadian forces. All the landings were successful and on only one beach did the Germans

Opposite **Air-view of amphibious vehicles landing on the shore of Northern France on "D-Day."**

inflict heavy casualties on the invaders. By evening the Allies had gained a firm foothold on northern Europe. Rommel's counter attack had not materialized.

On 4th June meteorological reports had indicated that the rough seas would prevent an invasion during the following fortnight. Many key officers had taken the opportunity to leave their posts and were absent when the invasion took place. Rommel himself had been away, hoping to persuade Hitler to send another Panzer division to Normandy. He did not get back to his headquarters until evening, by which time he had missed the chance to organize an immediate counter attack.

This apart, the German system of command on D–Day was in a state of chaos. Some troops were under Rommel's command, others under Rundstedt, and yet others were under Hitler's personal instructions. Valuable time was lost because the junior commanders were not given orders. One panzer division which might have dealt a serious blow to the invaders remained immobile – no-one dared move it without Hitler's permission, and he was asleep until late in the morning.

Rommel had been right about the effect of Allied air power. The reinforcements needed to make large detours due to the number of bridges that had been destroyed by bombing. On the march they were attacked again and again by R.A.F. fighters and bombers. In one place the roads and fields were covered with destroyed equipment, dead men and dead pack animals. General Eisenhower later said that "it was possible to walk for hundreds of yards at a time stepping on nothing but dead and decaying flesh."

When the belated reinforcements finally arrived bit by bit at the front they were immediately thrown into defence in an attempt to contain the Allies' ever-increasing bridgehead. In the following days and weeks the Germans were never able to amass a force large enough to launch the counter attack Rundstedt had hoped for. The effect of Allied air power was so devastating that the Allies were able to send reinforcements to Normandy by sea more quickly than the Germans could send their reinforcements by land.

There was little Rommel could do. He later said, "[My] functions in Normandy were so restricted by Hitler that any sergeant-major could have carried them out." Two weeks after D-day both Rommel and Rundstedt were agreed that Normandy could not be held. They tried to persuade Hitler to sanction a withdrawal, but the deluded Fuehrer was insistent that his forces hold their ground. Inevitably, the Allied build-up continued until, on 31st July, they broke out and flooded across France and Belgium sweeping all before them.

By this time Rommel was no longer burdened with command. He had become one of the many casualties of the battle. On 17th July his car had crashed after being shot at by one of the enemy aircraft which continually attacked German transport. Rommel's skull had been fractured, and there seemed little hope of saving his life. Ironically the incident occurred near a French village named Sainte Foy de Montgommery.

> "Restricted by Hitler in the deployment of his tanks, uncovered in the skies, short of men and arms, he never had in Normandy the opportunity for creative generalship *on the battlefield*. There his role was one of desperately plugging holes."
> Ronald Lewin. Rommel as Military Commander.

Left **General Montgomery (right) stopping on a road in France to watch German prisoners marching past.**

15. The Plot Against Hitler

In the first stage of the war Hitler's military decisions had been very astute. For the spectacular fall of France the Fuehrer could claim much of the credit – indeed, in the date and plan of attack he had not been supported by the senior members of the German High Command. But from the time of the evacuation of Dunkirk his decisions became increasingly open to criticism – although military experts disagree upon which of his decisions were right and which were wrong.

After 1942, when the invading German Army in Russia began to falter, Hitler became increasingly irrational, until, by the end of the war, his military directives indicated positive madness.

Rommel had never had much respect for Nazis in general, but he tended to regard Hitler as being a cut above his followers – he thought of the Fuehrer as an idealist. And the respect he felt for Hitler as a man and a military leader increased during the campaigns in Poland and France. Irritation set in with the North African campaign. The Desert Fox was greatly put out by Hitler's inability to see the importance of the North African war and his refusal to furnish the necessary troops. But it was not until Alamein that Rommel's real disillusionment began. Hitler could not stand the thought of the slightest reverse. Refusing to sanction a retreat became a mania with him – hence his extra-

Opposite **Adolf Hitler**

ordinary demand to stand firm at Alamein.

On 28th November, 1942, Rommel went to see Hitler in order to obtain permission to withraw from the untenable position at Mersa Brega. He had expected reasonable discussion, but he found that when he mentioned the possibility of withdrawal from Africa "the Fuehrer flew into a fury and directed a stream of completely unfounded attacks upon [the Africa Corps]." This interview had a tremendous impact on Rommel. This was a side of the German leader he had never seen before: "I began to realize that Adolf Hitler simply did not want to see the situation as it was, and that he reacted emotionally against what his intelligence must have told him was right." Rommel's futile attempt to persuade Hitler to evacuate the troops from the hopeless situation in Tunisia completed his disillusionment.

Back from his "Gentleman's War" in North Africa, Rommel began to learn about the atrocities the Nazis were committing in Europe. According to one authority Rommel "went straight to Hitler himself with these discoveries. 'If such things are allowed to go on,' he said 'we shall lose the war.' He then proposed the disbandment of the Gestapo and the splitting of the S.S. among the regular forces." But Hitler made it quite clear to Rommel that he had no intention of changing his methods. Despite the fact that he was not politically minded, Rommel became increasingly convinced that Hitler would be the ruin of Germany. Finally, he found himself drawn into a conspiracy to overthrow the man he had once respected.

For many years a group of high-ranking German officers and a few civilians had been plotting against Hitler. They had made plans to kill him on a number of occasions, but each time they had been foiled before they could put their plans into operation. The conspirators were concerned not only with getting rid of Hitler, they

"After Hitler himself, Rommel was probably the most popular man in Germany. Politically there was nothing against him. He had, indeed, to his own annoyance, been built up by the propagandists as a good Nazi. At the same time he was known to be respected by the British, with whom, at the crucial moment, he would have to treat. Outside a small circle, no-one knew that he was at cross-purposes with the Fuehrer. He was, therefore, the obvious choice, indeed the the only one." *Desmond Young. Rommel.*

also wanted to form a non-Nazi government and bring the war to an end. To do this they needed a supporter who was popular both at home and abroad. Nobody could have fitted their requirements better than Rommel. He was one of the most popular men in Germany at the time, well respected by the Allies, and he did not keep his opinions of Hitler a secret.

Rommel's first meeting with one of the conspirators took place in February, 1944. From then on he remained on the fringes of the plot. He never in fact knew that the conspirators intended to kill Hitler, but expected them merely to arrest him and bring him to trial. At this time most Germans still had great faith in their Fuehrer and Rommel felt that if Hitler was assassinated he would become a martyr to the German people.

To the conspirators, however, the only way to overthrow Hitler was to kill him. The climax of all this intrigue came when one of them planted a bomb in Hitler's conference room – it went off, but the explosion failed to kill the Fuehrer. Worst still, the attempted military coup that followed was a complete failure, and most of those conspirators that did not commit suicide were rounded up, put on trial, and brutally executed.

While all this had been going on, Rommel had been undergoing medical treatment. Although he made a remarkable recovery from his wounds he was not to live much longer. On 13th October 1944, while convalescing at his home, Generals Burgdorf and Maisel arrived at his home and asked to speak to him in private.

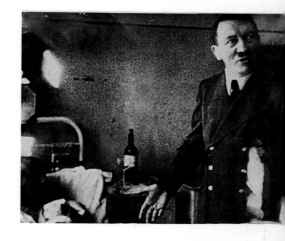

Above **Adolf Hitler visiting the people injured during the attempt on his life, 1944.**

16. The Perfect Soldier

Throughout his entire adult life, Rommel had taken little interest in anything other than his profession. His military activities apart, he seems to have been a rather ordinary man, very single-minded. He had no interest in the arts, he drank very little, good food and luxuries meant nothing to him. Occasionally he liked to go shooting or fishing, but other than that he had few pastimes.

An extremely practical man, Rommel soon developed a contempt for the "armchair soldiers" by whom he was much criticized. Although the theoretical tacticians and strategists have a place in any army, they always require a man like Rommel to fight the battles – war rarely goes according to plan. Rommel was in every sense "a fighting general" with all the qualities essential in a military leader – courage, drive, imagination and determination.

As a theorist he has been more open to criticism. The Atlantic Wall has been regarded as complete folly by many military writers and Rommel, although he did not instigate it, sought to complete the construction. However, the Atlantic Wall never *was* completed, and as Rommel could not put his theories into practice history cannot be the judge.

As far as Rommel's tactical ability is concerned, we know that this was masterful. Few people have questioned Rommel's talent for getting the most out of his

Opposite **Rommel.**

men and matériel on the battlefield. For this alone he will surely be remembered as one of the greatest military leaders of the century.

Being concerned with the practical, with things rather than ideas, Rommel had little interest in politics, except insofar as it affected the military situation. Nazi propaganda made out that he had been an early member of the Nazi Party, but this was untrue. He had nothing but contempt for the brownshirts, the S.S. and the other sinister trappings of the Nazi state. Rommel's convictions were moral, not political. The soldierly virtues of patriotism, loyalty and obedience were at the root of his personality.

He was in fact the perfect soldier. Not the type who merely seeks promotion, but a man who, after Hitler presented him with his Field Marshal's baton, remarked to his wife, "I would rather he had given me one more division."

Below **Rommel (second from left) seated on a car somewhere in Libya.**

Principal Characters

Auchinleck, Claude John Eyre. British General and later Field Marshal. In 1941 he was appointed Commander-in-Chief Middle East. He took over command of the Eighth Army after the defeat at Gazala and Tobruk and managed to hold Rommel at Alamein.

Guderian, Heinz. German General. After service in the First World War he became known as an expert in armoured warfare. He was the leading advocate of Blitzkrieg before the Second World War, and its leading exponent in the Polish, French and Russian campaigns.

Hitler, Adolf (1889–1945). The leader of the Nazi Party. Became Chancellor of Germany in 1933 and Dictator in 1934. He declared war on Poland in 1939 and thereby instigated the Second World War.

Montgomery, Bernard Law (1887–). British Field Marshal who took command of the Eighth Army in August, 1942. Defeated Rommel at Alamein and drove the Panzer Army out of Egypt and Libya. He commanded the Allied forces during the invasion of Normandy and later a British army group during the subsequent advance into Germany.

Mussolini, Benito (1883–1945). Dictator of Fascist Italy.

Rundstedt, Karl Rudolf Gerd von. German Field Marshal of aristocratic birth. Rose to high rank between the wars and commanded an army group during the Polish, French and Russian campaigns. Later appointed Commander-in-Chief West.

Wavell, Archibald Percival. British General and statesman, appointed Commander-in-Chief Middle East in 1939. He launched an offensive against the Italians which drove them out of Cyrenaica. His forces were in turn driven back to Egypt by Rommel's newly arrived Africa Corps. Wavell later became Viceroy of India.

Table of Dates

1891 Birth of Erwin Rommel.

1910 Rommel joins the 124th Infantry Regiment.

1912 Rommel receives his commission as an officer.

1914 Beginning of the First World War and Rommel's first combat.

1916 Rommel marries.

1917 German offensive in the Isonzo.

1918 End of the First World War.

1928 Rommel's son, Manfred, is born.

1937 Rommel publishes his book, *Infantry Attacks*.

1939 German invasion of Poland: beginning of the Second World War.

1940 German invasion of the West. Rommel commands the 7th Panzer division. Italian offensive in Egypt. British counter offensive and Italian rout in Libya.

1941 German troops under Rommel's command arrive in Africa. Rommel's first ofiensive in North Africa.

1942 Battle of Gazala. Fall of Tobruk, Panzer Army reaches the Alamein Line. Rommel's furthest advance in Africa. Eighth Army begins its attack at Alamein. Rommel begins to retreat.

1943 End of Axis resistance in North Africa.

1944 Rommel meets with conspiritors against Hitler. D-Day: the Allied invasion of Northern Europe. Rommel seriously wounded after his car is attacked by enemy places. Rommel is forced to commit suicide.

Further Reading

Hart, B. H. Liddell. *History of the Second World War* (Cassell, 1970). Liddell Hart was an eminent military theorist as well as an historian. The Blitzkrieg tactic was largely his invention, but it was disregarded in Britain until the Germans used it with such devastating effect. In this book he gives an excellent account of the war. It is rather long but for anyone who wants a true understanding of the subject it is well worth reading.

Rommel, Erwin. *The Rommel Papers*. Edited by B. H. Liddell Hart (Collins, 1953). Rommel's own record of his part in the defeat of France and the war in Africa. The book is well edited to give a comprehensive account of his military activities during the last war. Difficult to follow if one does not have some knowledge of military terms and the war in general.

Young, Desmond. *Rommel* (Fontana Books, 1955). Desmond Young served with the British Army in Africa and was eventually captured by the Africa Corps. This very readable biography gives one a good idea what fighting in the desert was like for Rommel and for his enemies. It contains a lot of information about Rommel's personal life as well as his military exploits.

Index

Picture Credits

The author and publishers wish to thank all those who have given per-
mission to reproduce copyright illustrations on the following pages:
Popperfoto, 8, 30, 36–37, 41, 46, 50–51, 58–59, 70, 83, 90; Radio Times
Hulton Picture Library, 12, 15, 16, 18, 20, 22, 26, 87; the Mansell
Collection, 42, 60, 64, 72, 78, 80; the Imperial War Museum, 29, 38, 44,
48, 52, 84, 88; Keystone Press Agency, 66, 71, 75, 76, 78.